ANALOGIES
FOR YOUNG
KIDS

BOOK 1
by Jan Zebrack

Helping Local Kids

**ALL THE PROFITS FROM THIS BOOK
BENEFIT THE
CHILDREN'S MIRACLE NETWORK HOSPITALS**

For Jerry Zebrack M.D.

Copyright © 2014 Jan Zebrack
All rights reserved
ISBN: 061586838X
ISBN 13: 9780615868387
Library of Congress Control Number: 2013915113
Bedrock, Reno, NV

Summary: Introduces the concept of analogies in a fun and engaging way; expands a child's knowledge of our culture.

All photos by Jan Zebrack, unless otherwise noted.
Cover and back cover photos courtesy of Gregory Popovich, Comedy Pet Theater, Las Vegas, NV

TABLE OF CONTENTS

NOTE TO TEACHERS AND PARENTS..................................iv

CULTURE

A bridle is to a horse 1

A soccer ball is to soccer 3

Sticks are to a drum 5

A human baby is to a human mother's sling 7

Hugs are to a smile 9

Sheep are to a shepherd 11

A steering wheel is to a car 13

A telephone wire is to a land-line phone 15

A teacher is to a school 17

White is to a bride in America 19

WORDS OF POSITION

Left is to right 23

Right-side up is to upside down 25

A hot-air balloon is to up 27

MATH

An octagon is to a spider..31

The size of one button is to the size of a bathtub 33

Ten dimes are to a dollar 35

One-sixth is to one-third 37

15 minutes are to 60 minutes 39

YOUR PAGE TO CREATE 41

NOTE TO TEACHERS AND PARENTS

THIS BOOK HAS FOUR BENEFITS:

1. **An outstanding balanced education includes having students use their analytical skills to develop critical and creative thinking.** These are essential elements in a complete education. One of our greatest strengths as a nation is our ability to innovate. This book can ignite your imagination and that of your students. This is not your traditional book on analogies. The reader isn't always limited to finding one right answer; with some of the analogies, several related answers may be appropriate. This gives the student an opportunity to explain his or her answer. Analogies are important because they change the way we think, read and write about the world. Learning analogies will not only benefit students in school, but throughout their lives by helping them see relationships between subjects. Grasping analogies is important for students at all levels of academic learning. For example, the Miller Analogies Test (MAT) is used for admission to hundreds of programs in college graduate schools; sometimes it is used instead of the Graduate Record Examinations, and other times it is the only test required.

2. **The book is an entertaining educational tool designed to engage young readers.** In introducing topics such as culture, math and words of position, the book features analogies and illustrative photographs that expose students to items from cultures and environments from around the world.

3. **The book fosters creativity.** It offers the student an opportunity to prove his or her understanding of the concept of analogies by entering a contest on "Your Page to Create" at the end of the book. There, the student can write his or her original analogy and a hint, then illustrate all four parts. Students who "think outside the box' are the ones who go on to find cures for diseases, compose music, create art, develop inventions, and found businesses such as Apple, Amazon, Microsoft or Facebook.

4. **The book benefits a worthy cause.** One hundred percent of the profits from this book go to the Children's Miracle Network Hospitals_ the leading hospital network in the United States for the treatment of sick and injured children.

Culture

A BRIDLE is to a HORSE,

as a LEASH is to ...

(What animal uses a leash?)

ANSWER: a dog.

A bridle is used to guide a horse.
A leash is used to guide a dog.

PHOTO OF DOG, GREGORY POPOVICH, OWNER OF COMEDY PET THEATER, LAS VEGAS, NV

A soccer BALL is to SOCCER,

as a SADDLE is to ...

(Hint: What sport is a saddle used for?)

ANSWER: horse back riding.

You need a soccer ball to play soccer.
You need a saddle to ride a horse.
This horse is jumping a fence.
What sport do you love?

PHOTO OF SOCCER PLAYER, JENNY ZEBRACK M.D., RENO, NV
PHOTO OF HORSE: JULIA PIVOVAROVA/SHUTTERSTOCK.COM

STICKS are to a DRUM,

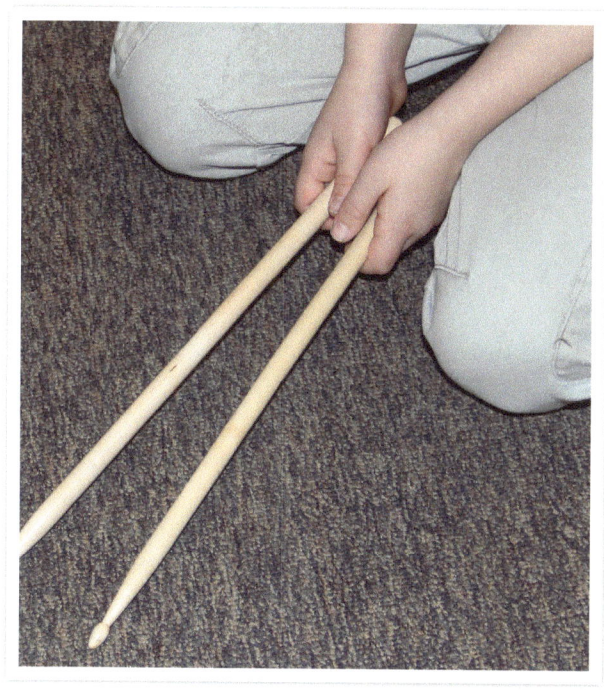

as PEBBLES are to ...

(Hint: What instrument uses pebbles to make music?)

ANSWER: maracas.

You can use sticks to make music on a drum.
You can use pebbles inside maracas to make music.
All music has rhythm. Most music also has melody.
Music brings great joy to people all over the world.
Would you like to learn to make music?

PHOTO OF MARACAS, GENGIRL/SHUTTERSTOCK.COM

A human BABY is to a human mother's sling,

(UGANDA, AFRICA)

as a JOEY is to his kangaroo mother's …

(Hint: A joey is a baby kangaroo.)

ANSWER: pouch.

(AUSTRALIA)

A human mother can carry her baby in a sling.
A kangaroo mother can carry her joey in a pouch.

PHOTO OF HUMAN BABY, LINDA CLIFT, RENO, NV
PHOTO OF KANGAROO, IDIZ/SHUTTERSTOCK

HUGS are to a SMILE,

(SILVER SALMON CREEK, ALASKA)

as HITTING is to ...

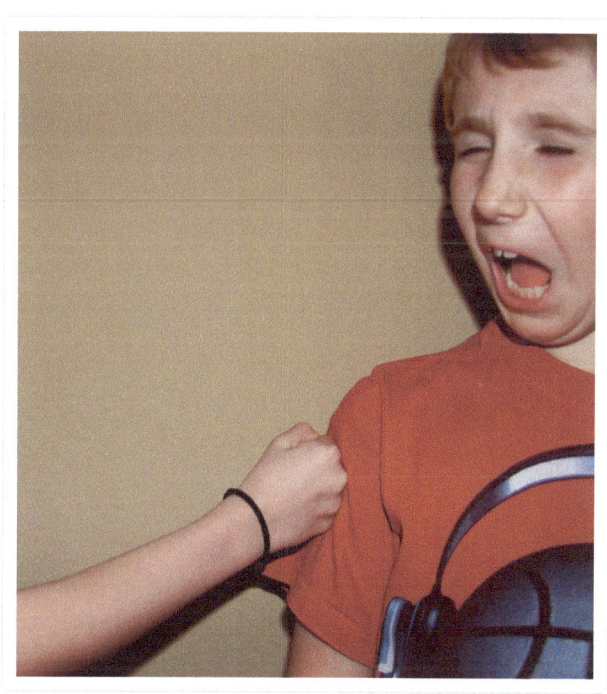

(Hint: What do little kids do when they are hurt?)

ANSWER: cry.

Hugs make us feel good. Hitting makes us very sad or scared. People who hit us, or say mean things to make us feel bad, are bullies. Have you ever been bullied? Do you know someone who has? Being kind is more important than being cute or pretty. Treat other people as you would like to be treated.

PHOTO OF GIRL CRYING, DAN WALDECK, LAFAYETTE, CO
PHOTO OF GIRL SMILING, MARY BROWN, SANTA ROSA, CA
PHOTO OF BEARS, DIANE MCALLISTER, RENO, NV

SHEEP are to a SHEPHERD,

(INDIA)

as COWS are to ...

(Hint: Who takes care of cows?)

ANSWER: a cowboy.

(CALIFORNIA, USA)

A shepherd takes care of sheep.
A cowboy takes care of cows.

PHOTO OF SHEPHERD, LINDA CLIFT, RENO, NV

A STEERING WHEEL is to a CAR,

as HANDLEBARS are to ...

(Hint: What do you steer with handlebars?)

ANSWER: a bicycle.

While driving a car, you steer with a steering wheel. While riding a bike, you steer with the handlebars. What kind of car do you like?

A TELEPHONE WIRE is to a LAND LINE PHONE,

as a CELL TOWER is to ...

(Hint: What phone uses the signal from a cell tower?)

ANSWER: a cell phone.

A land-line phone gets its power from the lines on a telephone pole. A cell phone gets its signal from a cell tower. Who would you like to call? What would you talk about?

A TEACHER is to a SCHOOL,

as a DOCTOR is to ...

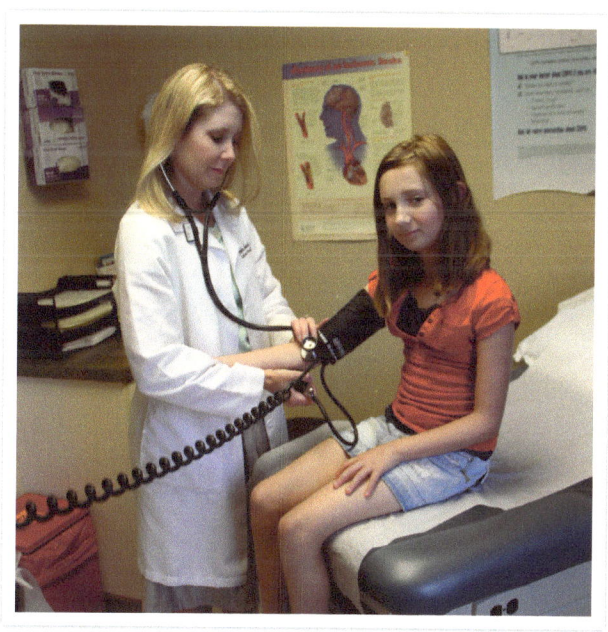

(Hint: Where does a doctor work?)

ANSWER: a hospital.

(RENO, NV)

Teachers work in schools, teaching students.
Doctors work in hospitals, treating patients.

What would you like to be when you grow up?
"Whatever you are, be a good one."

—Abraham Lincoln

WHITE is to a BRIDE in America,

as RED is to a BRIDE in ...

(Hint: This country is located in Asia and starts with the letter C.)

ANSWER: China.

(PING AN, CHINA)

The traditional color for brides to wear in America is white. The traditional color for brides to wear in China is red. Some brides in India, Pakistan and Vietnam also wear red.

PHOTO OF BRIDE IN RED COURTESY, JASON GU, PING AN, CHINA
PHOTO OF BRIDE IN WHITE, KRIS NASH, RENO , NV

Words of Position

Up

Words of Position

Down

LEFT is to RIGHT,

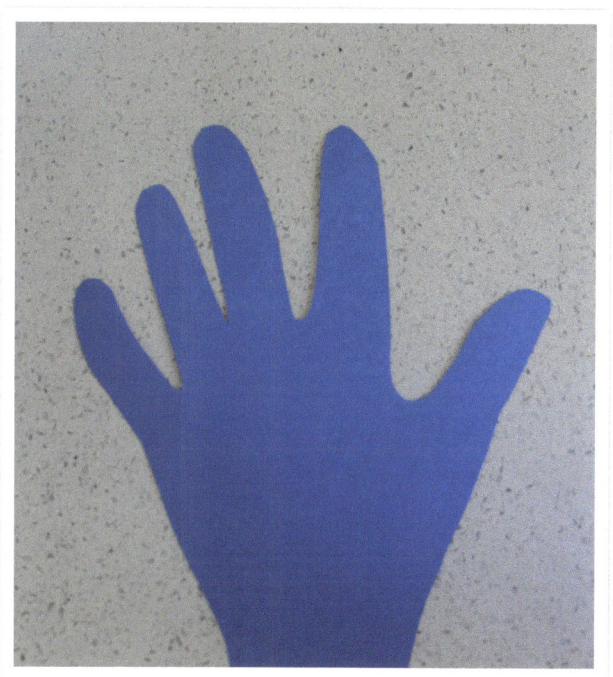 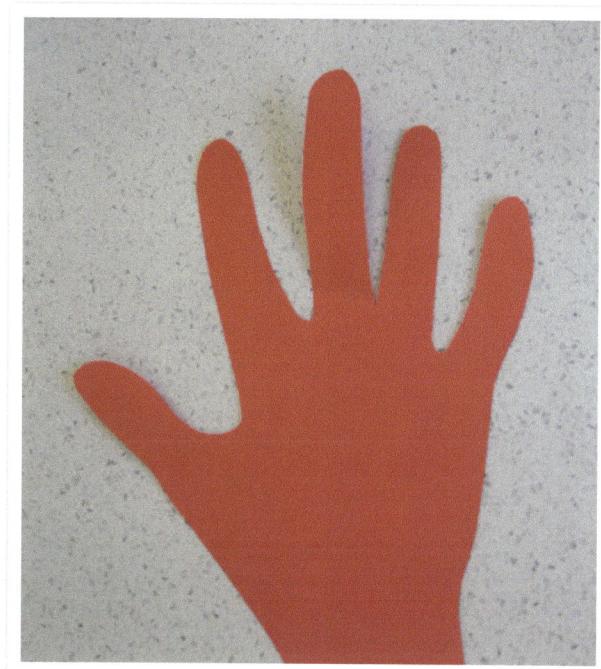

as ABOVE is to ...

(Hint: What is the opposite of above?)

ANSWER: below.

(NEVADA DESERT)

The red hand is the **right** hand.
The blue hand is the **left** hand.
You start to read and write on the left side of the paper. How many students write with their left hand in your class?

PHOTO OF OLD CAR, TREVOR OXBORROW, INCLINE, NV

RIGHT-SIDE UP is to UPSIDE DOWN,

as FRONT is to ...

(Hint: What is the opposite of front?)

ANSWER: back.

Right-side up is the opposite of upside down.
Front is the opposite of back.
Can you stand on your hands so
you are upside down?

A HOT-AIR BALLOON RISING is to UP,

(RENO BALLON RACES)

as a WATER SLIDE is to ...

(SQUAW VALLEY, CALIFORNIA)

(Hint: What is the opposite of up?)

ANSWER: down.

Gas that is lighter than air
makes air balloons go up.
Gravity makes kids come down a water slide.

Draw a picture of yourself going up into space
or write a story about it.

PHOTO OF HOT-AIR BALLOON, DAN WALDECK, LOUISVILLE, CO

Math

GEOMETRIC SHAPES

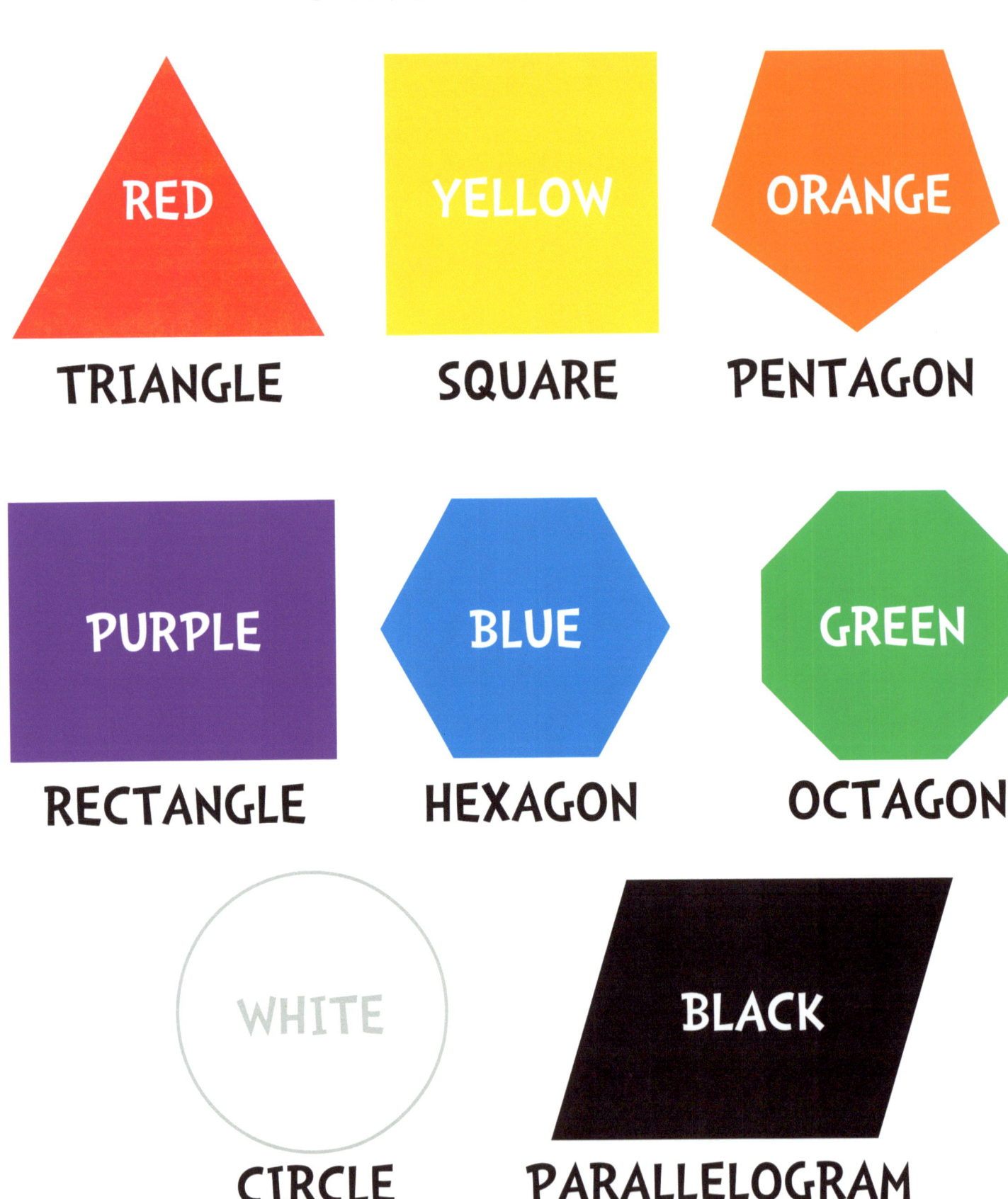

An OCTAGON is to a SPIDER

as a HEXAGON is to an ...

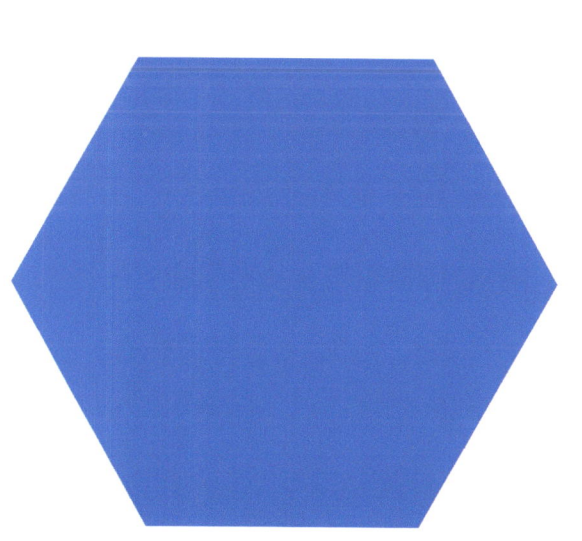 

(Hint: What animal has six legs?)

ANSWER: insect.

An octagon has eight sides.
A spider has eight legs.
A hexagon has six sides.
An insect has six legs.
How would you make a drawing with only octagons, hexagons or triangles?

Photo credit: geometric shapes: Enka Parmu/Shutterstock.com
Photo credit: spider, Diane McAllister, Reno, NV
Photo credit: insect, MongPro/Shutterstock.com

The SIZE OF ONE BUTTON is to the SIZE OF A BATHTUB,

as the SIZE OF 80 BUTTONS is to the size of ...

(Hint: What holds water and is about 80 times as big as a bathtub?)

ANSWER: a swim pool.

A swim pool is about 80 times as big as a bathtub.

Photo Of Bathtub Courtesy Of Port D'hiver Bed And Breakfast, Melbourne Beach, Florida

10 DIMES are to a DOLLAR

as 10 NICKELS are to ...

(Hint: What coin is worth ten nickels?)

ANSWER: a 50 cent coin.

Ten dimes are equal to a dollar.
Ten nickels are equal to a 50 cent coin.
A 50 cent coin is also called a half-dollar.
Do you earn money with an allowance?
Why are you saving money?

ONE-SIXTH is to ONE-THIRD

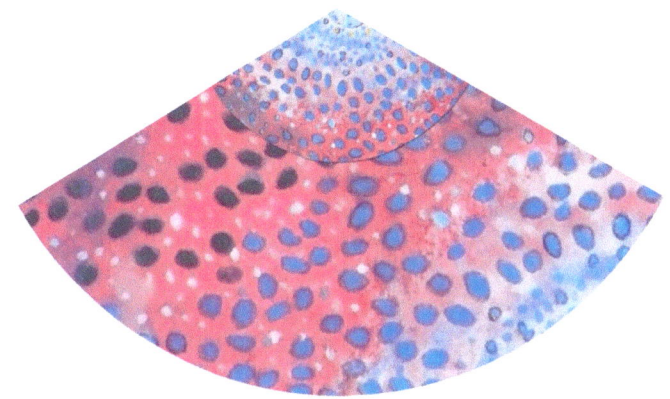

as ONE-HALF is to ...

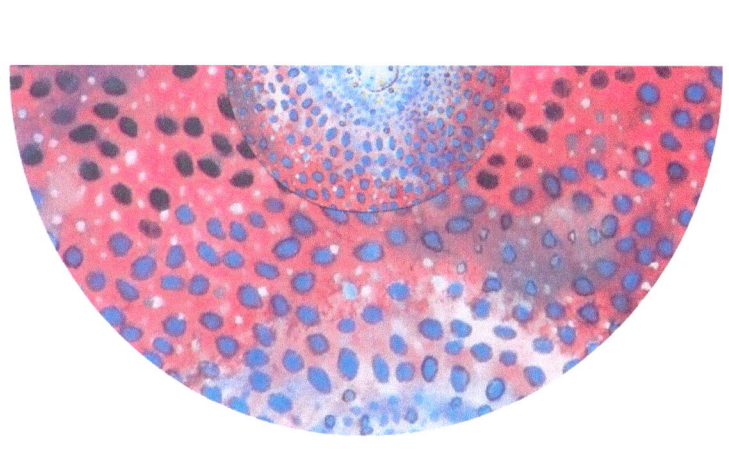

(Hint: One-third is twice as big as one-sixth.)

ANSWER: a whole.

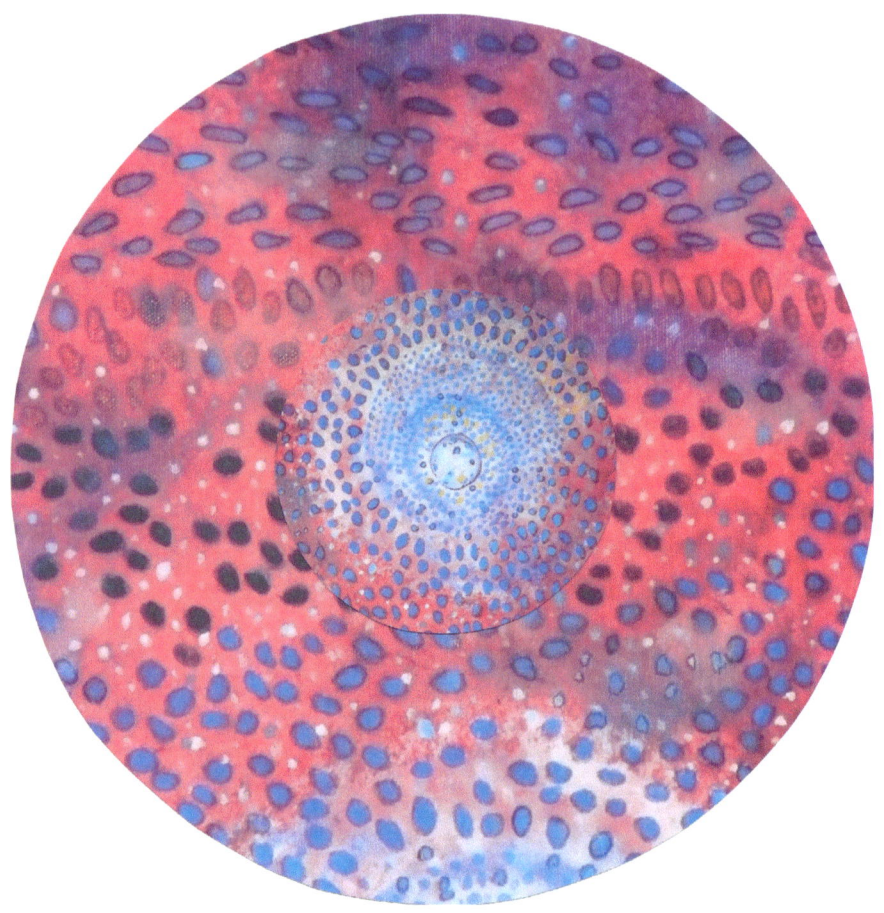

One-sixth plus one-sixth equals one-third.
One-half plus one-half equals a whole.
How many things with the shape
of a circle can you imagine?

ART CREDIT: TONI LOWDEN, RENO, NV

15 MINUTES are to 60 MINUTES,

as a QUARTER is to ...

(Hint: 15 minutes are equal to 1/4 of an hour.)

ANSWER: a dollar.

15 minutes is a quarter of an hour.
15 minutes times four equals 60 minutes.
A quarter of a dollar is worth 25 cents.
25 cents times four equals a dollar.

How do you imagine a place with no clocks or money? How would life be different?

YOUR PAGE TO CREATE

Pages 41, 42, 43 and 44 are places for you to write and draw an analogy that YOU make up. The pattern should be: A_____ is to B_____ as C_____ is to D_____. Be sure your analogy has one logical answer. Related answers may be appropriate. Draw with colored markers four objects, animals, plants or people to illustrate your analogy. Draw with colored markers or paint four objects, animals, plants or people to illustrate your analogy. Each painting should be on a separate sheet of 8 1/2 by 11 inch paper.

Photograph or scan each sheet, including the analogy. Sign the form on page 40 and email a scan of it and of the four sheets of your analogy drawings to janetzebrack@yahoo.com as an attachment, OR mail entry to: Jan Zebrack, 216 Lemmon Drive Box 385, Reno, NV 89506

Your entry will be considered for a $100 prize to be awarded each month for the first year of publication to your school. You can write an analogy on any subject you choose. Awards will be based on the originality of the analogy and the artistic quality of the art. Each month's winner will be shown on www.AuthorJanZebrack.com and included in a book titled:

"ANALOGIES WRITTEN AND ILLUSTRATED BY KIDS"

Only your first name, age, teacher, school, city and state will be published in the book and website.

Your analogy: _____
_____
Hint: (to help kids figure out your analogy.)

Your name _____
Your age _____
Name of your teacher _____
Name of your principal _____
Name of your school _____
Address of your school _____

Please sign below and include this form with your analogy, hint and artwork. I am the parent or legal guardian of this child _____ and I give permission for my child's analogy and drawings to appear in the book titled: **ANALOGIES WRITTEN AND ILLUSTRATED BY KIDS.**

SIGN _____

DATE: _____

ALL THE PROFITS FROM THIS BOOK WILL GO TO THE CHILDREN'S MIRACLE NETWORK HOSPITALS.

The Children's Miracle Network is a non-profit organization working with 170 children's hospitals in the United States and Canada to help kids recover from illness or accidents.

www.ingramcontent.com/pod-product-compliance
Lightning Source LLC
Chambersburg PA
CBHW042123040426
42450CB00002B/45